How to Make Money on YouTube

Complete Guideline for Beginner to Expert Step by Step

Disclaimer

The publisher and author disclaim all responsibility for the content of this book, including any errors, omissions, or discrepancies. The book is provided "as is" and only for informational purposes. The results achieved by following the tips and techniques contained in this book may vary depending on the individual reader. The samples and references included in this book showcase some of the remarkable results that are possible but are not guaranteed or assured.

Copyright © Kevin Marquez 2022

All rights reserved. No part of this book may be reproduced, stored in a retrieval system, or transmitted in any form or by any means, electronic, mechanical, photocopying, recording, or otherwise, without prior written permission of the copyright owner.

Contents

INTRODUCTION 4

YOUTUBE FUNDAMENTALS 5

PLANNING 8

EQUIPMENT 13

CREATING YOUTUBE CHANNEL 17

YouTube Studio Details 24

YOUR APPEARANCE 25

YOUTUBE SHORTS 29

UPLOADING VIDEO 31

LIVE STREAMING 38

ANALYTICS 40

GETTING MORE SUBSCRIBERS 42

MAKING MONEY 45

INTRODUCTION

Are you interested in becoming a YouTuber? Do you want to learn how to upload videos, optimize them for maximum views, and make money from your YouTube channel? If so, this book is for you!

You'll learn everything you need to know about being a successful YouTuber, from choosing the right niche and equipment to filming and editing your videos, to promoting your channel and monetizing your content.

You'll also get practical tips and advice on everything from building a loyal fanbase to growing your channel and increasing your earnings.

So, if you're ready to learn how to be a successful YouTuber, this book is for you!

YouTube Fundamentals

How Does YouTube Make Money?

YouTube makes money through a variety of mechanisms, the most prominent of which is advertising. YouTube offers two types of advertising: cost-per-impression (CPM) and cost-per-click (CPC). Advertisers can choose which type of advertising they want to run on their videos, and they can also set a budget for how much they are willing to spend.

CPM advertising is the type of advertising where advertisers pay based on the number of views that their ad receives. CPC advertising is the type of advertising where advertisers pay based on the number of times that users click on their ad. YouTube also offers ad-free subscription options for users who do not want to see ads on the platform.

In addition to advertising, YouTube also generates revenue through YouTube Red, its premium subscription service. YouTube Red allows users to watch videos without ads, as well as access exclusive content that is not available on the free version of the platform. YouTube also generates revenue through the sale of merchandise, such as t-shirts and other branded items.

How Do You Make Money from Youtube?

Making money from YouTube is a multi-faceted approach. The most popular method is through ad revenue, but there are also other ways you can make money from the platform.

Ad revenue is generated through ads that are displayed on your videos. You get a portion of the ad revenue based on how many views your video gets. The more views, the more money you make.

You can also make money through sponsorships. Companies will pay you to promote their products in your videos. This can be done through verbal mentions, visual placements, or both.

Another way to make money from YouTube is through merchandising. You can sell branded merchandise through your channels, such as t-shirts, mugs, and other items. This is a great way to make money if you have a large and engaged audience.

Finally, you can also make money from YouTube through affiliate marketing. This is where you promote a product or service in your video and get a commission for every sale that you generate. This can be a great way to make money if you have a niche channel with an engaged audience.

So, there are a few different ways that you can make money from YouTube. Ad revenue is the most popular, but there are also other options available.

You Need to Know YouTube Algorithm Properly

The YouTube algorithm is a set of rules that determines what videos are shown to users on the site. The algorithm is designed to promote videos that are popular and relevant to users, while also keeping the site fresh with new content.

The algorithm takes into account a number of factors when determining which videos to show users, including the number of views, likes, and comments a video has, as well as how long ago it was uploaded. The algorithm also looks at the user's viewing history to determine what kinds of videos they might be interested in.

YouTube makes frequent changes to its algorithm, in order to improve the user experience on the site. The company has said that its goal is to show users the videos they're most likely to find interesting and engaging.

As a YouTuber, it's important to understand how the YouTube algorithm works so that you can make the most of it. The algorithm is constantly changing and evolving, so it's important to keep up-to-date with the latest changes.

There are a few key things that you can do to make sure your videos are as visible as possible on YouTube. Firstly, make sure your videos are well-optimized and include relevant keywords in the title and description. This will help YouTube to understand what your video is about and match it with relevant searches.

Secondly, interact with your viewers and encourage them to leave comments and like your videos. This sends positive signals to YouTube that your video is engaging and worth watching.

Finally, promote your videos across other social media platforms and on your website or blog. This will help to drive traffic to your videos and increase their chances of being seen by YouTube users.

By following these tips, you can ensure that your videos are more likely to be seen by YouTube users and appear higher up in search results. This will help you to build a loyal following and grow your channel.

Planning

Find Your Channel Topic

If you want to be successful on YouTube, it is essential to have a clear and consistent channel topic. This will help you attract viewers who are interested in your content, and it will also help you build a strong and loyal following. But how do you find your channel topic? Here are a few tips:

1. Know your audience. The first step to finding your channel topic is to understand your audience. Who are you making videos for? What are their interests? What are their needs? Once you have a good understanding of your audience, you will be able to identify potential topics for your channel.

2. Do your research. Once you have an idea of the types of videos your audience wants to see, it is time to do your research. Look at other popular YouTube channels and see what topics they cover. You can also use YouTube's keyword tool to find out what people are searching for.

3. Be unique. There are already a lot of channels on YouTube, so it is important to be unique. Find a niche that you can fill and that will set you apart from the rest.

4. Be passionate. When you are passionate about your topic, it will show in your videos. This will make your videos more enjoyable to watch and it will also help you build a stronger connection with your viewers.

5. Be consistent. Once you have found your channel topic, it is important to be consistent. Stick to that topic and don't veer off into other areas. This will help you build a loyal following of viewers who know what to expect from your channel.

Branding

As a YouTuber, it's important to have a strong and consistent brand. This not only applies to your videos, but also to your channel page.

Your channel page is the first thing viewers see when they visit your channel, so it's important to make a good first impression. Here are some tips for branding your channel page:

1. Use a strong profile picture. This is the first thing people will see, so make sure it's a good representation of you and your brand.

2. Use a catchy channel description. This is your chance to tell viewers what your channel is all about. Make it clear, concise, and engaging.

3. Use a consistent color scheme. This will help your channel look professional and cohesive.

4. Use high-quality visuals. This includes your channel banner, thumbnails, and videos.

5. Use keywords in your tags and titles.

By following these tips, you can create a strong and consistent brand for your YouTube channel. This will help you attract more viewers and build a successful channel.

Unique Video Style

There's no doubt that video is one of the most powerful and popular forms of content out there. But with so much competition, how can you make sure that your videos stand out from the rest?

One way to ensure that your videos are unique is to develop a specific style that is unlike any other. Creating a unique video style can be a challenge, but with some careful research, it is achievable. There are a few key things to consider when researching a unique video style. Firstly, what is the purpose of the video? What message are you trying to communicate? Once you have a clear idea of the purpose of the video, you can begin to look at different styles and see which one would best suit your needs. Secondly, who is your target audience? It is important to consider who will be watching the video and what type of style would appeal to them. Lastly, what is your budget? Depending on the budget, you may need to be more creative with your approach to creating a unique video style.

Once you have considered all of these factors, you can begin to research different video styles. A good place to start is by looking at other videos that have been created for similar purposes. This will give you an idea of what has been done before and what is possible. You can also look at different filmmakers and see what styles they have used in their work. This can be a great way to get inspiration for your own unique video style.

Once you have an idea of the different styles that are available, you can start to experiment and see what works best for your video. Remember, the goal is to create something that is unique and will appeal to your target audience. With some careful research and experimentation, you can create a video style that is truly your own.

Find your Unique Video Making Plan

You need a video-making plan that's unique to you and your goals. There's no one-size-fits-all approach to video making, so it's important to find a plan that works for you. Here are a few things to keep in mind as you formulate your plan:

1. What are your goals?

Are you trying to promote a product or service? Drive traffic to your website? Increase brand awareness? Your goals should be specific and measurable. This will help you track your progress and determine whether or not your video-making plan is working.

2. Who is your target audience?

Who is your target audience for your videos? What are their demographics? What are their interests? Knowing your target audience will help you create videos that are more likely to resonate with them.

3. What type of videos do you want to make?

There are many different types of videos you can make, from educational videos to product demonstrations to entertaining videos. Figure out what type of videos will best help you achieve your goals.

4. What equipment do you need?

You don't need a fancy camera or editing software to make great videos. However, you will need some basic equipment, such as a tripod and a microphone. If you're planning on filming yourself, you may also want to invest in a good lighting setup.

5. How often will you make videos?

Some businesses release new videos on a weekly basis, while others only create videos occasionally. Figure out what schedule works best for you and your team. There's no right or wrong answer here, but consistency is key.

Creating a video-making plan is the first step to achieving your video marketing goals. By taking the time to figure out what you want to achieve and how you're going to achieve it, you'll be in a much better position to create videos that actually deliver results.

EQUIPMENT

Introduction

Making high-quality YouTube videos requires good equipment. Even if you have great editing skills, if your videos are grainy or have poor sound quality, viewers will likely not stick around.

Good equipment doesn't have to be expensive, but it should be able to produce clear and crisp images and sound. A good camera is essential for filming your videos. You'll also need a microphone to ensure that your audio is clear.

Investing in good equipment will make a big difference in the quality of your videos. It will also make the video-making process more enjoyable, as you won't have to worry about poor footage or audio ruining your videos. let's deep down.

Cameras

There are many reasons why you might need a high-quality camera for YouTube videos. Perhaps you want to start a channel and need to invest in good equipment, or maybe you've been making videos for a while but want to upgrade your gear to get better results. Whatever the case, having a good camera can make a big difference in the quality of your videos.

One of the most important things to consider when choosing a camera for YouTube is the resolution. Many people watch videos on HD TVs or monitors, so you'll want to make sure your camera can output in at least 1080p. This will ensure that your videos look sharp and clear on larger screens. You might also want to consider a camera that can shoot in 4K, as this is the future standard for video resolution.

The size of the sensor is another important factor to consider. A larger sensor will allow you to shoot in low light conditions without sacrificing image quality. This is especially important if you plan on shooting indoors or in other dimly lit situations.

Finally, you'll want to make sure the camera you choose has good autofocus and image stabilization. This will help you keep your shots steady and in focus, even if you're moving around or the camera is shaking. These features are especially important if you're shooting a video with a lot of movement.

There are a lot of great cameras on the market, so it's important to do your research and find the one that's right for you. With a good camera, you can take your YouTube videos to the next level and get the results you're looking for.

Audio

If you want your YouTube videos to sound professional, you need to use high-quality audio. This doesn't mean that you need to spend a lot of money on expensive equipment. There are many affordable ways to get great-sounding audio for your videos.

One reason why you need high-quality audio for your YouTube videos is that it will help you to stand out from the competition. There are millions of videos on YouTube, and many of them have poor-quality audio. If your videos sound great, they'll be more likely to catch people's attention and get views.

Another reason to use high-quality audio is that it will make your videos sound more professional. This can help you to attract more viewers and subscribers, as well as get more opportunities to collaborate with other YouTubers.

Finally, good audio is essential for creating an engaging and enjoyable viewing experience. If your audio is poor, people will have a hard time understanding what you're saying or following your video. This can lead to people getting frustrated and clicking away from your video.

So, if you want your YouTube videos to sound their best, make sure to use high-quality audio. There are many affordable ways to get great audio for your videos, so there's no excuse not to. Your viewers will appreciate it, and you'll be more likely to achieve success on YouTube.

Lighting

There are many benefits to using good quality lighting when making YouTube videos. Perhaps the most obvious benefit is that it makes your videos look more professional. This can help you attract more viewers and subscribers, as well as lead to more opportunities for collaboration and sponsorship.

Good lighting can also make your videos more enjoyable to watch. Poor lighting can be harsh and unflattering, while good lighting can make people look and feel their best. This is especially important if you are making videos that are meant to be inspiring or educational, as you want your viewers to feel positive after watching them.

Finally, good lighting is essential for ensuring that your videos are clear and easy to see. This is especially important if you are making how-to videos or other types of videos that require your viewers to be able to see what you are doing. If your lighting is poor, your viewers may have difficulty following along, which can lead to frustration and eventually cause them to stop watching your videos altogether.

Editing

If you want to know how to edit your YouTube video, there are a few things that you will need to do. First, you will need to find a video editing program that you can use. There are many different programs out there, so you may want to take some time to research which one will work best for you. Once you have found a video editing program, you will need to download it and install it on your computer.

Once you have the video editing program installed on your computer, you will need to open the program and load your YouTube video into it. Once your video is loaded into the program, you will be able to edit it however you like. You can cut out parts of the video that you do not want, you can add effects, and you can even add music to the video.

Once you have edited your video the way that you want, you will need to save it.

There are a number of popular video editing tools available on the market today. Here are a few of the most popular options:

Adobe Premiere Pro: Adobe Premiere Pro is a widely used video editing tool that offers a variety of features and options for users. It is compatible with both Windows and macOS.

Final Cut Pro: Final Cut Pro is another popular video editing tool, available for macOS only. It offers a variety of features and options for users and is often used by professional video editors.

Avid Media Composer: Avid Media Composer is a widely used video editing tool that offers a variety of features and options for users. It is available for Windows and macOS both.

DaVinci Resolve: DaVinci Resolve is a popular video editing tool that offers a variety of features and options for users. It can be used on both Windows and macOS.

CREATING YOUTUBE CHANNEL

How to Create a YouTube Channel

Creating a YouTube channel is a great way to share your video content with a wide audience. You can create a channel for free, and it only takes a few minutes. Here's how:

1. Go to youtube.com and sign in with your Google Account. If you don't have a Google Account, you can create one now.

2. Click on the "My Channel" link in the left sidebar.

3. Enter a name for your channel and click "Create Channel."

4. You'll be taken to your new channel's page. From here, you can add videos, playlists, and other information.

5. To add videos, click the "Upload Videos" link in the left sidebar.

6. You can also add videos by clicking the "Upload Videos" button on your channel's page.

7. To add a playlist, click the "Add to Playlist" button on any video that you want to include in the playlist.

8. You can also create a new playlist by clicking the "Create Playlist" button on your channel's page.

9. Once you've added videos and playlists, you can start customizing your channel's look and feel. To do this, click the "Edit Channel" link in the left sidebar.

10. You can also find more information about how to create and manage your YouTube channel by visiting YouTube's Help Center.

Channel Art

Creating a great YouTube channel art can be key to attracting new viewers and subscribers to your channel. Here are some tips to help you get started:

1. Decide on a theme or style for your channel art. This will help you determine the overall look and feel of your channel.

2. Choose a template or create your own design. There are many templates available online that you can use as a starting point for your channel art.

3. Use high-quality images and graphics. This will help your channel art stand out and look professional.

4. Use colors that match your brand or style. This will help create a cohesive look for your channel.

5. Keep your channel art simple and clean. Too much clutter can be overwhelming and turn viewers away.

6. Make sure your channel art is the right size. YouTube has specific size requirements for channel art, so make sure your artwork meets those requirements.

7. Test your channel art before you publish it. This will help you ensure that everything looks the way you want it to.

Creating great YouTube channel art can help you attract new viewers and subscribers to your channel. By following these tips, you can create channel art that is professional, stylish, and sure to impress.

Channel Description

Are you looking for ways to improve your channel and get more views? If so, then you need to learn how to write a channel description. A channel description is a short paragraph that appears below your channel name and is one of the first things that viewers see when they visit your channel.

Your channel description should be concise and to the point. It should give viewers an idea of what your channel is about and what they can expect to find. Avoid using long, run-on sentences or too much technical jargon. Instead, focus on creating a description that is easy to read and understand.

When writing your channel description, be sure to include keywords that describe your channel content. These keywords will help viewers find your channel when they are searching for specific topics. For example, if your channel is about cooking, you may want to include keywords such as "cooking," "recipes," and "food."

In addition to including keywords, your channel description should also be engaging and well-written. This means using proper grammar and spelling, as well as avoiding any type of clickbait or misleading information. You want viewers to stick around after they visit your channel, so make sure your description is accurate and enticing.

writing a channel description may seem like a lot of work, but it's worth it if you want to attract more viewers to your channel. By following the tips above, you can create a description that accurately reflects your channel content and helps you get more views.

Channel Layout

There are a few key features to look for when considering the layout of your YouTube channel. The first is to make sure your channel is easy to navigate. You want your viewers to be able to find the content they're looking for quickly and easily. There should be a clear hierarchy to your content, with the most important information being prominently displayed.

Another important consideration is the overall branding of your channel. Your channel layout should reflect the overall tone and personality of your brand. It should be visually appealing and consistent with the rest of your marketing materials.

Finally, you'll want to consider how often you'll be updating your channel. If you plan on regularly adding new content, you'll want to make sure your channel layout is easy to update. You don't want your viewers to get frustrated with a cluttered or outdated channel.

By considering these factors, you can ensure that your YouTube channel layout is effective and reflects the overall tone of your brand.

Channel Trailer

As a YouTuber, your channel trailer is one of the first things new viewers will see when they come to your channel. This makes it a crucial part of your channel branding and one of the most important videos on your channel.

A channel trailer should be short, sweet, and to the point. It should give viewers a taste of what your channel is all about and make them want to subscribe.

Here are some tips for making an awesome channel trailer:

1. Keep it under 2 minutes.

The average attention span of a person is only 8 seconds, so you want to make sure your channel trailer is short and sweet. 2 minutes is the perfect length for a channel trailer.

2. Start with a bang.

Your channel trailer should start with a bang to grab attention and keep viewers hooked. Start with your most exciting or popular video.

3. Introduce yourself.

Be sure to introduce yourself in your channel trailer. Tell viewers your name, what your channel is about, and why they should subscribe.

4. Use graphics and music.

Make your channel trailer visually appealing by adding graphics and music. This will help it stand out and make it more memorable.

5. Promote your best stuff.

Use your channel trailer to promote your best content. This is a great way to get new viewers interested in what you have to offer.

By following these tips, you can create an awesome channel trailer that will help brand your channel and attract new subscribers.

Monetization

For monetization eligibility you need to see youtube's latest guideline on the creator studio.

If you meet these requirements, you can apply to monetize your channel. Once you're approved, you can start earning money from ads on your videos.

There are a few things to keep in mind when you're monetizing your videos. First, you need to make sure that your content is advertiser-friendly. That means avoiding profanity, sexual content, and other topics that may not be appropriate for ads.

Second, you need to make sure that your videos are high quality and engaging. If your videos are low quality or boring, viewers will not watch them, and you will not make any money.

Third, you need to be consistent in uploading videos. If you only upload a few videos, you will not get many views, and you will not make much money.

If you keep these things in mind, you can start earning money from your YouTube channel.

Copyright

If you upload videos to YouTube, you need to be aware of the copyright policy. This policy outlines what you can and cannot upload, as well as the consequences of violating the policy.

The first thing to note is that you can only upload videos that you have the rights to. This means that you either need to own the video or have permission from the copyright holder. If you upload a video that you do not have the rights to, it will be taken down and you may face legal action.

YouTube also has a policy against "spam, deceptive practices, and scams." This means that you cannot upload videos that are intended to mislead or trick people. This includes videos that are clickbait or that make false claims. If your video is removed for violating this policy, you may also face legal action.

Finally, YouTube has a three-strike policy for copyright violations. This means that if you upload a video that violates copyright, you will receive a strike. If you receive three strikes, your account will be terminated. This policy is designed to protect copyright holders and to ensure that only videos that are legally allowed to be on YouTube are uploaded.

If you are planning on uploading videos to YouTube, it is important to be aware of the copyright policy. By understanding the policy, you can avoid having your videos removed or your account terminated.

YouTube Studio Details

As a content creator on YouTube, it's important to understand how to use the YouTube Studio Dashboard. This is the place where you can manage your YouTube channel, upload videos, and track your channel's analytics. In this article, we'll give you a tour of the Dashboard and show you how to navigate it.

The YouTube Studio Dashboard is divided into four main sections: Home, Analytics, Upload, and More.

The Home section is where you can see an overview of your channel. This includes your channel's subscribers, views, and watch time. You can also access your channel's settings from here.

The Analytics section is where you can track your channel's performance. This includes your channel's views, watch time, and demographics. You can also see which of your videos are performing well and which ones need improvement.

The Upload section is where you can upload new videos to your channel. You can also manage your video settings, including your thumbnail, description, and tags.

The More section is where you can access additional features, such as YouTube Live, YouTube Red, and YouTube TV. You can also find help and support from here.

Now that you know how to navigate the YouTube Studio Dashboard, let's take a look at some of the things you can do from here.

As a content creator, you can use the Dashboard to:

Upload new videos

Edit your video settings

Track your channel's analytics

Check your channel's subscriber count

See your channel's watch time

Find help and support

As you can see, the YouTube Studio Dashboard is a powerful tool that can help you manage your channel and grow your audience. So, be sure to explore it and take advantage of all it has to offer.

YOUR APPEARANCE

You have always loved entertaining people. You've been the life of the party since you were a kid. When you were in school, you were always the one cracking jokes and making everyone laugh. You loved being the center of attention. Now that you're an adult, you've decided to take your love of entertaining people and turn it into a career. You're going to be a YouTuber.

You know that to be a successful YouTuber, you need to be good at a few things. You need to be a good storyteller, you need to be funny, you need to be a good actor, and you need to be a good presenter. Fortunately, you excel at all of these things. You're confident that you can be a successful YouTuber.

The first step to becoming a successful YouTuber is to create interesting and engaging content. You need to be able to tell a story that will captivate your audience. You also need to be able to make your content funny. People love to watch videos that make them laugh. You need to be able to keep your audience entertained.

The second step to becoming a successful YouTuber is to be a good actor. You need to be able to convincingly act out the scenes in your videos. If your acting is bad, people will not want to watch your videos. You need to be able to make your audience believe that you are the character you are playing.

The third step to becoming a successful YouTuber is to be a good presenter. You need to be able to keep your audience engaged. You need to be able to answer questions and interact with your audience. You need to be able to keep your audience interested in what you're saying.

If you can master these three things, you will be well on your way to becoming a successful YouTuber.

Your Perfect Appearance

To be a YouTuber, you don't have to be perfect, but you do have to look presentable. Here are some tips on how to make sure your appearance is up to par:

1. Wear clothes that are appropriate for your audience. If you're making videos for a family audience, avoid wearing anything too revealing or provocative. Likewise, if you're aiming for a more mature audience, you don't want to dress too juvenile.

2. Make sure your hair is clean and styled. This may seem like a no-brainer, but you'd be surprised how many people neglect their hair when they're filming videos.

3. Wear minimal makeup. You don't want to look like you're wearing a mask of makeup, so keep it light and natural.

4. Be aware of your body language. Avoid crossing your arms or slouching, as this can make you appear closed off or unconfident.

5. Smile! This will make you appear more approachable and likable.

By following these tips, you can be sure that you're putting your best foot forward in your videos. Remember, people are more likely to watch and enjoy your content if they think you're a likable person. So, make sure your appearance is conveying the right message.

Looking Presentable

If you're a YouTuber, then you know how important it is to look presentable on camera. After all, your audience is watching you for entertainment and education, so you need to make sure you look your best. Here are some tips on how to look presentable for a YouTuber:

1. Dress the part. Depending on your niche, you'll want to dress accordingly. If you're a gaming YouTuber, you might not need to dress up as much as someone who's a beauty vlogger. Find a style that works for you and stick with it.

2. Make sure your hair and makeup are on point. This is especially important for female YouTubers. Take the time to do your hair and makeup before you start filming. It will make a world of difference.

3. Be aware of your body language. Sit up straight, make eye contact with the camera, and use your hands to emphasize your points. Avoid fidgeting or looking away from the camera too much.

4. Smile! This might seem like a no-brainer, but it's important to remember to smile when you're on camera. It will make you seem more friendly and approachable.

5. Be yourself. This is the most important tip of all. You need to be comfortable and confident in front of the camera, and the only way to do that is to be yourself. Don't try to be someone you're not. Just be yourself and the rest will fall into place.

YouTube Shorts

YouTube Shorts is a new short-form video feature on YouTube that allows users to create and share 15-second videos. YouTube Shorts provides a new opportunity for YouTubers to create engaging, shareable content that can be easily consumed on the go.

With YouTube Shorts, YouTubers can earn money in a variety of ways. Ad revenue will still be generated from views on YouTube Shorts videos, and YouTubers can also monetize their videos through YouTube's Partner Program. In addition, YouTube is also rolling out a new "superchat" feature that allows fans to donate money to their favorite YouTubers while they are live streaming.

Overall, YouTube Shorts provides a new and exciting opportunity for YouTubers to create content and earn money. With a variety of ways to monetize their videos, YouTubers can start earning money from their YouTube Shorts videos right away.

How to Upload YouTube Shorts

YouTube Shorts are a new way to create and watch short, engaging videos on YouTube. Here's how to upload your own YouTube Shorts:

Step 1: Open the YouTube app on your phone.

Step 2: Tap on the camera icon in the top right corner.

Step 3: Select "Create a new short" from the options.

Step 4: Choose how you want to record your video. You can record directly from the app, or upload a video from your phone's library.

Step 5: Once you've recorded or uploaded your video, edit it using the various tools available. You can trim your video, add filters, music, and more.

Step 6: When you're happy with your video, tap on "Next".

Step 7: Choose a thumbnail for your video and add a title.

Step 8: Tap on "Publish" to upload your YouTube Short.

How Shorts are Discovered on YouTube

There are a few ways that shorts are discovered on YouTube. The most common is through YouTube channels that feature shorts. These channels typically have a large following and showcase a variety of shorts from different creators.

Another way shorts are discovered on YouTube is through algorithmically generated recommendations. YouTube's algorithm is constantly watching what users are watching and recommending similar videos. This means that if a user watches a lot of shorts, they're likely to see more shorts in their recommendations.

Finally, shorts can also be discovered through social media. YouTube creators often share their shorts on other platforms like Twitter and Instagram. This can help them reach a wider audience and get more views.

Uploading Video

Title

It's no secret that YouTube is one of the largest search engines in the world. In fact, it's the second-largest search engine after Google. That's why it's so important to make sure your YouTube videos are optimized for SEO.

One of the most important aspects of SEO is your video title. Your title is what appears in the search results, so it needs to be attention-grabbing and relevant to your video. Here are some tips for writing an SEO-friendly title for your YouTube videos:

1. Keep it short and sweet.

Your title should be short and to the point. It should be no more than 60 characters, and it should accurately describe what your video is about.

2. Use your keywords.

Your title should include your keywords so that your video can be easily found when people search for those terms. However, don't stuff your title with keywords; use them judiciously.

3. Make it readable.

Your title should be easy to read and understand. Avoid using abbreviations or jargon that people might not be familiar with.

4. Use proper grammar.

This should go without saying, but your title should be well-written and free of any grammar or spelling errors.

5. Be creative.

Your title should be creative and unique. Avoid using generic titles like "How to [X]." Be specific and describe what your video is about in an interesting way.

By following these tips, you can write an SEO-friendly title for your YouTube videos that will help them rank higher in the search results.

Description

As a YouTuber, it's important to make sure your videos are properly optimized for SEO. This includes creating an interesting and keyword-rich title, as well as a description that will entice viewers to watch your video. Here are some tips on how to write an SEO-friendly description for your YouTube videos:

1. Use keywords in your title and description.

Make sure to use relevant keywords in your title and description, as this will help your video show up in search results. Try to use long-tail keywords, which are more specific and less competitive than short-tail keywords.

2. Keep your description short and to the point.

Your description should be short and sweet, as viewers are more likely to watch a video that is straight to the point. Try to include the most important information in the first sentence, as this is what will show up in search results.

3. Use a call to action in your description.

Encourage viewers to watch your video by using a call to action in your description. For example, you could say "For tips on how to improve your SEO, watch this video."

4. Use rich media in your description.

Make your description more visually appealing by adding rich media, such as images, infographics, or even a video thumbnail. This will help your video stand out in the search results.

5. Optimize your thumbnail image.

Your thumbnail image is important for two reasons: first, it will show up in the search results, and second, it will be the first thing that viewers see when they click on your video. Make sure to choose an attention-grabbing image that accurately represents your video.

By following these tips, you can write an SEO-friendly description for your YouTube videos that will help them rank higher in the search results and get more views.

Thumbnail

As a YouTuber, one of the most important things you can do to make your channel successful is to create engaging and eye-catching thumbnails for your videos. Here are some tips on how to make noticeable thumbnails for your YouTube videos:

1. Use bright and contrasting colors. This will help your thumbnail stand out from the other videos on the YouTube homepage.

2. Use an interesting or unique image. This will help your thumbnail to be noticed and clicked on by potential viewers.

3. Use text to highlight the title or main message of your video. This will help viewers to understand what your video is about before they even click on it.

4. Keep your thumbnail simple and easy to understand. This will help viewers to quickly see what your video is about and decide whether or not they want to watch it.

By following these tips, you can create thumbnails for your YouTube videos that are both eye-catching and informative. This will help to increase your views and subscribers, and ultimately make your channel more successful.

Tags

There are a few ways to find tags for a YouTube video. The first way is to look at the tags that are already associated with similar videos. To do this, go to YouTube and search for a video that is similar to the one you want to tag. Then, look at the tags that are associated with that video.

Another way to find tags for a YouTube video is to use a keyword research tool. There are a number of different keyword research tools available, but some of the most popular ones are Google AdWords Keyword Planner and WordStream. To use either of these tools, simply enter a keyword that is relevant to your video and see what words and phrases come up. These are all potential tags for your video.

Finally, you can also ask people who have watched your video what they think the best tags for it are. This can be done by leaving a comment on the video itself or by sending out a survey to your viewers. Either way, you should be able to get some good ideas for tags from the people who have already seen your video.

Category

There are a few things to consider when selecting a category for your YouTube video. The first is to think about what type of content your video falls under. This can help you to decide which category is the best fit. For example, if your video is a vlog, then the 'People & Blogs' category would be a good choice. If your video is a tutorial, then the 'How-to & Style' category would be a better option.

Another thing to consider is the audience you are trying to reach with your video. YouTube has a wide range of categories, so you should think about which one your target audience is most likely to watch. For example, if you are trying to reach a younger audience, then the 'Music' or 'Gaming' category would be a good choice. If you are trying to reach a more mature audience, then the 'News & Politics' or 'Education' category would be a better option.

Finally, you should also consider the keywords you are using to promote your video. This can help you to decide which category is most relevant to your video. For example, if you are using the keyword 'cat', then the 'Pets & Animals' category would be a good choice. If you are using the keyword 'tutorial', then the 'How-to & Style' category would be a better option.

Remember, there is no right or wrong answer when it comes to selecting a category for your YouTube video. The most important thing is to choose a category that is relevant to your video and that will reach your target audience.

Privacy Settings

There are a few simple steps you can take to make sure your YouTube videos are as private as possible. First, log in to your YouTube account and click on the "Settings" icon in the top right corner. In the "Privacy" section of the settings menu, you can choose to make your videos "Public," "Unlisted," or "Private."

If you select "Public," your video will be visible to anyone who visits your YouTube channel. "Unlisted" videos can be seen and shared by anyone who has the link, but they won't appear in any public search results. "Private" videos can only be seen by people who you invite to view them.

You can also control who can comment on your videos. In the "Comments" section of the privacy settings, you can choose to allow comments from anyone, only people you know, or no one at all.

Finally, you can decide whether or not to allow other YouTube users to add your video to their playlists. If you select "No," only you will be able to add your video to a playlist.

By taking a few minutes to adjust your privacy settings, you can make sure that your YouTube videos are only seen by the people you want to see them.

Captions

Adding captions to your YouTube video is a great thing, there are some easy ways. You can do it yourself using a text editor, or you can use a captioning service.

If you want to do it yourself, the first thing you need to do is create a transcript of your video. This can be done by transcribing the audio of your video, or by writing out what is being said in the video.

When you have a transcript of your video, you can then create the captions using a text editor. You will need to create a separate caption file for each language that you want to include.

When you have created the caption files, you need to upload them to YouTube. To do this, go to the YouTube video manager and select the "Subtitles/CC" tab. From here, you can upload your caption files.

If you want to use a captioning service, there are a few different ones to choose from. One option is Rev.com. With this service, you can upload your video and they will create the captions for you.

Another option is to use a tool like Amara.org. With this tool, you can create the captions yourself, or you can have others do it for you.

When you have created the captions for your video, you can then add them to your video using the "Subtitles/CC" tab in the YouTube video manager.

Annotations

Annotations are a great way to add extra information to your YouTube videos. You can use them to point out key parts of the video, add links, or even add extra humor. Setting up annotations is easy and only takes a few minutes.

First, open the YouTube video editor by going to your video manager and selecting the "Edit" button. Next, click on the "Annotations" tab. Here you will see all the different annotation options.

To add an annotation, simply click on the type of annotation you want to add. For example, if you want to add text annotation, click on the "Text" option. A box will appear where you can type in your annotation.

Once you have typed in your annotation, you can adjust the size, color, and position of it. You can also add a link to another YouTube video or website.

Once you are happy with your annotation, click the "Save" button. Your annotation will now appear in your video.

LIVE STREAMING

People engage in live streaming on YouTube for a variety of reasons. Some people use it as a platform to share their talents with the world, while others use it as a way to connect with friends and family. Some people even use it as a way to make money.

Live streaming on YouTube is a great way to connect with friends and family who are scattered across the globe. It is also a great way to share your talents with the world. If you are a musician, for example, you can live stream your concerts and reach a wider audience. You can also use live streaming to provide tutorials, share your gaming skills, or even just have a conversation with people from all over the world.

You can make money by live streaming on YouTube. There are a few different ways to do this. One way is to become a YouTube Partner and make money through advertising. Another way is to sell products or services through your live stream. You can also accept donations from your viewers.

Analytics

YouTube Analytics is a tool that provides detailed information about your YouTube channel and videos. This information can help you improve your channel and videos so that they reach a larger audience.

There are several benefits to using YouTube Analytics. First, it can help you understand how people are finding and watching your videos. This information can be used to improve your marketing efforts. Second, YouTube Analytics can help you identify which videos are most popular with your audience. This information can be used to create more engaging and informative content. Finally, YouTube Analytics can help you track your progress over time. This information can be used to measure your success and identify areas for improvement.

YouTube analytics is a powerful tool that can help you improve your video content and grow your channel. By understanding your audience and what they want to see, you can create videos that will keep them engaged and coming back for more.

Here are a few things you can learn from your YouTube analytics:

1. Who is watching your videos?

You can see the demographics of your audience, including their age, gender, and location. This information can help you adjust your content to better appeal to your target audience.

2. What videos are they watching?

You can see which of your videos are being watched the most and for how long. This can help you understand what type of content your audience enjoys and wants to see more of.

3. When are they watching your videos?

You can see when your videos are being watched the most. This can help you determine the best time to release new videos and ensure that they are being seen by as many people as possible.

4. How are they finding your videos?

You can see how people are finding your videos, whether it be through search, social media, or other websites. This can help you adjust your marketing strategy to better promote your videos.

5. What devices are they using to watch your videos?

You can see what type of devices your audience is using to watch your videos. This can help you ensure that your videos are compatible with all devices and that they are being seen by as many people as possible.

YouTube analytics is a powerful tool that can help you grow your channel and improve your video content. By understanding your audience and what they want to see, you can create videos that will keep them engaged and coming back for more.

Getting More Subscribers

Trending Topic Videos

If you're looking to get more views on your YouTube videos, one of the best things you can do is to make videos on topics that are currently trending. This is because people are more likely to search for and watch videos on topics that are popular at the moment.

To find out what topics are currently trending, you can check out Google Trends or the trending section on YouTube. You can also use social media sites like Twitter to see what people are talking about.

Once you've found a few trending topics, try to come up with video ideas that would be popular with viewers. For example, if you're a gaming channel, you could make a video about the most popular games right now. Or if you're a beauty vlogger, you could do a tutorial on a trending makeup look.

Remember to make your videos engaging and entertaining, so that people will want to watch them. If you can get people to watch and enjoy your videos, they're more likely to share them with others, which will help you get even more views.

Networking and Collaborating

As a YouTuber, one of the most important things you can do to grow your channel is to network and collaborate with other creators.

This can help you get more subscribers in two ways: first, by increasing the visibility of your channel through cross-promotion, and second, by providing opportunities for your viewers to discover new content that they may enjoy.

Here are a few tips for networking and collaborating with other creators:

1. Join or create a YouTube Collaboration Group: There are many YouTube collaboration groups available online, or you can create your own. This is a great way to meet other YouTubers with similar interests and to get your channel in front of a new audience.

2. Participate in YouTube comment threads and forums: Engage with other YouTubers by leaving comments on their videos and participating in YouTube forums and discussion threads. This is a great way to start building relationships with other creators.

3. Collaborate with other YouTubers: One of the best ways to grow your channel is to collaborate with other YouTubers. This can be done by guest-starring in each other's videos, doing joint live streams, or even just promoting each other's content.

4. Attend YouTube events: There are often YouTube-focused events happening around the world, such as VidCon and Playlist Live. These are great opportunities to meet other creators and grow your network.

5. Use social media: Social media is a great way to connect with other YouTubers and promote your content. Follow other creators on Twitter, Facebook, and Instagram, and share their content on your own social media accounts.

Make a Series Consistently

If you want to get more subscribers for your YouTube channel, one of the best things you can do is create a series of videos. This will not only help to keep your viewers engaged, but it will also give them something to look forward to on a regular basis.

When creating a series, it is important to maintain a consistent theme or topic. This will make it easier for viewers to know what to expect from your videos and will also make it more likely that they will subscribe to your channel.

If you are having trouble coming up with ideas for your series, try thinking about topics that you are passionate about or that would be of interest to your target audience. Once you have a few ideas, start brainstorming ways to make each video unique and engaging.

Remember, the key to success on YouTube is to create content that your viewers will enjoy. If you can do that, you'll be well on your way to building a loyal following.

Scheduling Videos

If you want to get more subscribers to your YouTube channel, one of the best things you can do is schedule your videos. This means that you release a new video on a regular basis, preferably at least once a week. When people see that you are consistently putting out new content, they are more likely to subscribe to your channel.

Another benefit of scheduling your videos is that it can help you stay on track with your content creation. It can be easy to get sidetracked and start working on other projects, but if you have a schedule in place, it will be easier to stay focused on creating new videos.

If you are not sure how to get started with scheduling your videos, there are a few different ways you can do it. One option is to use a tool like Hootsuite or Buffer, which allow you to post your videos at a specific time and date. Another option is to manually upload your videos to YouTube at a specific time.

No matter which method you choose, the important thing is to be consistent with your video release schedule. This will help you build a loyal following of subscribers who will continue to watch your videos on a regular basis.

MAKING MONEY

There are many ways to make money with YouTube. You can become a YouTube Partner and make money from ads, create and sell your own products, or work with brands and businesses as an influencer.

As a YouTube Partner, you can make money from ads that are served on your videos. You will need to apply to become a Partner, and you will only be eligible if you have a certain number of subscribers and watch hours. Once you're a Partner, you can choose to run ads on your videos, and you will earn a percentage of the revenue from those ads.

You can also create and sell your own products on YouTube. If you have an idea for a product that you think people would want to buy, you can create a video about it and sell it on your YouTube channel. You can also work with brands and businesses as an influencer. If you have a large following on YouTube, you can approach brands and businesses and offer to promote their products or services on your channel. You can also offer to create sponsored videos for them.

YouTube Ads

Making money with YouTube ads is a great way to monetize your channel and earn some extra income. Here's a step-by-step guide on how to do it:

1. Sign up for a Google AdSense account. This is how you'll get paid for your YouTube ads.

2. Once you're approved, go to your YouTube video manager and click on the "Monetization" tab.

3. Enable monetization for your videos and agree to the terms.

4. Choose what kind of ads you want to run on your videos. You can choose from pre-roll, mid-roll, or post-roll ads.

5. Set a price for your ads. This is how much you'll get paid per view.

6. Once you've set up your account and chosen your ad settings, you're ready to start making money with YouTube ads!

YouTube ads can earn you a lot of money, depending on how many views your videos get. If you have a lot of views, you can make a lot of money from YouTube ads.

Affiliate Links

If you're looking to make money from affiliate links, there's no better place to start than with YouTube. You can create videos on just about any topic, and if you include affiliate links in your video descriptions, you can earn a commission on any sales that you generate.

To get started, you'll need to sign up for an affiliate program. Once you're approved, you'll be given a unique affiliate link that you can use in your video descriptions. When someone clicks on your link and makes a purchase, you'll earn a commission on the sale.

The amount of money you can earn from affiliate sales will depend on the products you're promoting and the commissions you're offered. For example, if you're promoting a product that costs $100 and you're offered a 10% commission, you'll earn $10 for every sale you generate.

To maximize your earnings potential, you should promote products that are in high demand and that offer high commissions. You should also create videos that are informative and engaging, as this will help to encourage viewers to click on your affiliate links.

Once you've built up a sizeable audience, you can also start to sell advertising space on your videos. This is another great way to earn money from your YouTube channel.

So, if you're looking to make money from YouTube, affiliate links are a great way to get started. Just be sure to choose products that are in high demand and offer high commissions, and create videos that are informative and engaging. With a little effort, you can start earning a nice income from your YouTube channel.

Sponsored Posts

YouTube offers a great way to make money from sponsored posts. By becoming a YouTube partner, you can make money from sponsorships, product placements, and other monetization opportunities.

To get started, you'll need to create a channel and start building an audience. Once you have a following, you can reach out to brands and businesses to pitch sponsorship opportunities.

To be successful, you'll need to create high-quality content that resonates with your audience and builds your brand. You'll also need to be strategic about the sponsors you choose to work with, making sure that they align with your values and offer products or services that your audience will be interested in.

By following these tips, you can start making money from sponsored posts on YouTube. With hard work and dedication, you can turn your YouTube channel into a lucrative business.

Selling Products

There's no doubt that YouTube has become a powerful platform with a global reach. And with that reach comes opportunities to make money. You can sell products through YouTube in a number of ways, and in this article, we'll explore some of the most effective methods.

One of the simplest ways to make money from selling products through YouTube is to include product links in your video descriptions. When viewers click on these links, they'll be taken to the product page on your website or online store. You'll earn a commission on any sales that result.

If you don't have your own products to sell, you can still make money by promoting products from other companies. For example, you could become an affiliate for a company and earn a commission on every sale you help generate. There are many companies that offer affiliate programs, and you can find them by searching online.

Another option is to sell products directly through YouTube. You can set up a shop on YouTube where viewers can browse and purchase your products. This is a great option if you have physical products to sell, such as clothing, jewelry, or art. You'll need to set up a payment system, such as PayPal, to process orders.

You can also sell digital products through YouTube. This could include items such as eBooks, courses, or software. You'll need to set up a way for viewers to download the products they purchase, such as through a link in the video description or a file-sharing service.

Finally, you can use YouTube to generate leads for your business. For example, you could create videos that provide valuable information related to your product or service. You can then include a call-to-action at the end of the video, such as a link to your website or a form to fill out to request more information.

There are many ways to make money from selling products through YouTube. By including product links in your video descriptions, becoming an affiliate for another company, or setting up a shop on YouTube, you can reach a wide audience and generate significant income.

www.ingramcontent.com/pod-product-compliance
Lightning Source LLC
Chambersburg PA
CBHW050315220526
45465CB00005B/2000